THE WONDERFUL WORLD
OF DR SLIDE
A BOOK OF RIDDLES FOR ALL

BY MICHAEL H. SCHECTER, MD

ISBN: 978-1-960146-85-4 (hard cover)
      978-1-960146-86-1 (soft cover)

Edited by: Erika Nein

Published by WARREN Publishing
Charlotte, NC
www.warrenpublishing.net
Printed in the United States

To my wife, Caline

I say to you, Welcome,
Come one and come all!
For this world is a wonder,
It's large and it's small.
A book full of riddles,
Some short and some tall,
The stories within often rhyme, but not all.

Please notice the QR code listed below.
Each riddle will have one, I think you should know.
So, check your solutions, perhaps you're the best,
To see how you did when compared to the rest.

Alas, some are tricky, a challenge at hand.
But before you give up, ask for hints if you can.
Enough of this intro, it's time to begin.
I hope you enjoy it and share with a friend!

Our host is a man;
dR slide is one name.
His interests are varied,
And he loves to make games.
But one in particular,
Better than most,
A poetic puzzle,
His namesake, our host.

Tell me his name and our journey begins!

At times I am a legend;
At others, just a note.
You use me every single day.
I'm often in your coat!

ABCDEFG,
But never H through Z.
If you're off, there's no hope
For peace and harmony.

A piece of information
As important as a clue.
Fail to pay attention,
And you won't know what to do.

Florida has so many,
And in your pocket ... at least two.

Superb musicians keep me
While enamored lovers share me.
But I'm sorry to say that you, my friend,
Won't always have me.

DIFFICULTY: 4

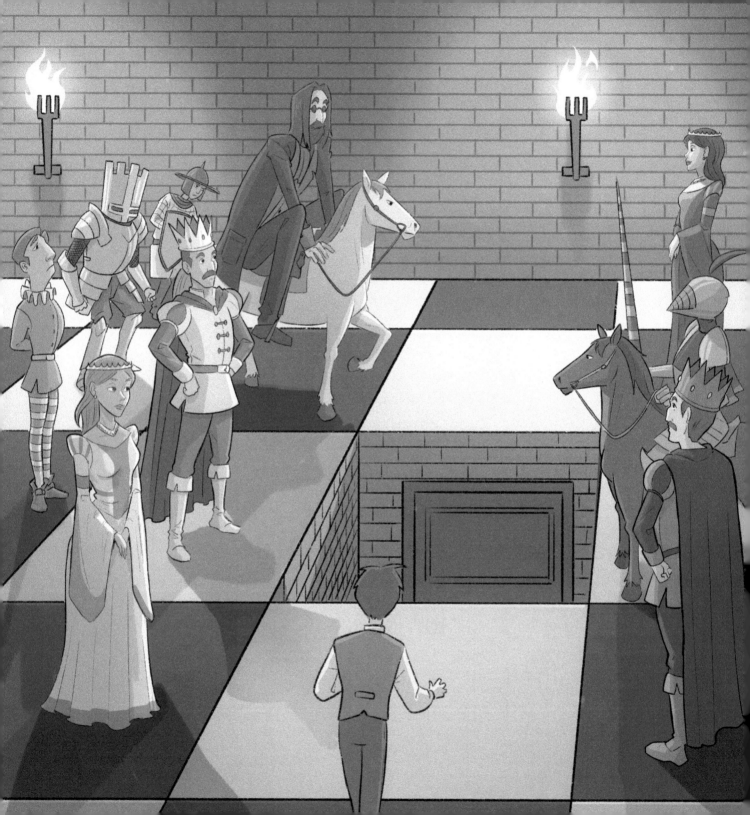

"I command this land in front of me,"
So says the king.
But seven steps in front of him,
A foe claims he's the king.
One black, one white;
Yet otherwise, their looks were but the same.
On checkered ground their armies fought
Until but one remained.

DIFFICULTY: 1

If only I could speak,
Oh, the things I would describe.
"Honey, I'm home!"
I would say as I arrived.
I'd tell stories of my garden
And my love for all the flowers.
I'd speak of giants that run
When they see me; some cower.

#6

It moves with no legs
And has an eye but can't see.
For this monster is dangerous
And sometimes deadly.

DIFFICULTY: 5

In some I am sharp as a tack;
In others, I am quite flat.
You and Count Dracula have me;
A letter and number, that's that.

DIFFICULTY: 4

I am not a compass,
But I orient you still.
I do not know the time of day,
But days of me you fill.

The first time you had me you cried.
Without me you wouldn't survive.
You control me and hold me
But sometimes can't catch me.
I frequently keep you alive!

DIFFICULTY: 3

Light is to dark
As I am to concrete …
A summary
And not much longer.

"Felon" is close, though I am not a criminal;
I'm furrier than many alternative animal.
I may steal your heart, though this isn't a crime—
My mischief endearing, my purring sublime.

DIFFICULTY: 1

To use my name in vain
Is to say you can't any longer.
For patience is a virtue,
Lift me up to make you stronger.

But do not carry me around
Like the world's burden on your shoulders.
With age you learn to do me better—
Wisdom granted when you're older.

In a sense, he claims to have it
And his motive is obscure,
His actions seem to be guilt ridden
What does he claim to have for sure?

And does he have that which he claims
The juror is unsure,
For our senses may deceive us
Sight and sound a whispered blur.

DIFFICULTY: 8

I know you know me,
So say my name,
Though temptation is
A dangerous game.

Some say I'm smooth,
I'm nimble and quick.
Don't play with me,
I'll make you sick.

My brothers three
Are all the same:
Heartless, except
The one that's sane.

Inside this box
I sit and wait,
But rest assured
I will escape.

I know you know me—
Say my name!

DIFFICULTY: 6

The highest of heights,
The tip of the top,
For I am a human
And prey a lot.

I do not have a mating call,
Though I do make quite a sound.
I fly but wings don't flap at all,
And I only like flat ground.

DIFFICULTY: 5

What is A - B - C + D?

Penny for your thoughts, your dreams,
Your deepest desires.
I'm showered with pennies
From all of you buyers.

Yet nobody asks what the cost is to sell.
With inflation and time,
You should pay me a dime.
And if not, then your dreams fare thee well!

DIFFICULTY: 5

I am not the news,
But the NEWS is what I tell.
I give you the location
Where the sun will set quite well.

I am not a demented bride
But my letters are the same.
Surgeons often do this thing
To keep diseases tame.

DIFFICULTY: 8

Say this is the life
As soon as you're here;
Just a slice of heaven,
And love without fear.

So, it sounds like we're Eden
When you say what we are;
No worries, no hurries,
An island afar.

An identical couple
Just tossed in the air;
As you gamble the odds with us …
3D squares.

DIFFICULTY: 7

I look like the number 0
But display it only once.
I display the number 1 five times
But the number 2 twice.
While numbers 3 through 9,
I display each once.

I command and you obey
More times than you do not.
I have no words to say,
But communicating colors is all I've got!

DIFFICULTY: 5

I become fixed when my reflex is broken ...
Call me a student, and you have misspoken.

DIFFICULTY: 7

In my presence you are mute
And sounds cannot escape.
And in my presence I may suck
But you can't breathe or vape.
Up above the world so high,
You'll find I have no shape.

Sometimes I watch you.
In the dark, I am gone.
I speak your language,
But you cannot hear me.

DIFFICULTY: 7

A series of numbers,
A riddle at hand,
A ubiquitous code,
That we use when we plan.
10, 6, 13, 1, 13, 10, 10, 1, 19, 15, 14, __

DIFFICULTY: 6

#28

Trapped behind glass
I count as I fall;
Composed of many particles
Discrete and small.

DIFFICULTY: 7

2 555 555
999 666 88
66 33 33 3
444 7777

DIFFICULTY: 7

Time is to wounds
As this is to bipolar.
Add: as what is to anemia,
And you have me—
The amalgamation.

#31

I roll out as a squad
Typically in groups of four,
Rarely alone and
Sometimes many more.
My shape is always constant
But I come in many sizes,
My motto, "Just go with the flow"
My fear: deflation, crisis!

DIFFICULTY: 6

Eleven, seventeen …
Luckily ubiquitous.
But I do not care
Because I am not sweet.

Where oh where
Could my pointy friend be?
My purpose: to help it fly free.
I know it's embedded
Within this, you said it,
So tell me its name properly!

DIFFICULTY: 8

A group was once known as her child;
Without free will, your fate beguiled.
Thought of often favorably;
Your future ... deterministically.

DIFFICULTY: 6

Automobile
A mondegreen within,
You can feel the change
As the air grows thin.

I'm not a car
And surely not a truck,
But if you're thinking fall
Then I think that you're in luck.

When spoken it means
That I give them the money
To borrow with interest … a loan.
And yet it has palm trees
And beaches a many
That the wealthiest people might own.

I am a tomb with exactly five corners.

To notice is to do it.
You hear it when I play it.
You make it when you might forget.
And when I teach ... you take it.

The nurses were worried,
The patient was ill.
The doc did **it** hurried,
Gave meds—all was chill!

The code master scrambled,
The combo obscure.
The numbers were sequenced,
He knew **it** for sure.

The courtroom was chaos,
The judge lost control.
She picked up her gavel,
And yelled **it** with soul.

DIFFICULTY: 3

All his pets have a very special diet
(Sometimes big and sometimes small)
And sometimes someone else will try it.
One ate nine for forty-one days
It's true, I can't deny it.
And two had five while one other had nine
Of this very special diet.

What almost always has two arms, two legs, and a head
But never has a face?

You can't contain me as I grow
Much larger by the second.
I've made the world around you
And I hope you find it pleasant.
If you're an adult,
Then I am when you were adolescent.
But time moves on; you can't stay long
As you become senescent.
Revisit me, I welcome you,
Though I am never present.

The value we place
On the thought of another
Is half of the value
We place on our own.

In total the cost
Of your opinion and mine
Must equal this
If it is known.

One foot is all I am,
Nothing more and nothing less.
But since you call me by my name,
Then that makes you my servant, yes?

Clever little puzzle poem
Solve it, if you dare.
Ten of us are: quick enough
And three of us are: rare,
Six of us are: in a box
Too small for the rest to share.
Jump up when you soon realize
We are all here, I swear.

Roses are red,
On occasion they're orange,
Yet sometimes you'll find one that's yellow.
Gentle and green,
Be the stem and sky blue,
Increasingly inching to indigo—
Vast and so violently violet.

You put fifteen into three edges
But you decide to spare me.
Then I'm compelled to beat the others
As your wrath, like lightning, strikes me.
I beat them 'til they're buried
Into one of the six graves.
Once beat on felt with all your touch
Thy will be done, I'm saved.

Once upon a time there was
A keyboard and a prince.
Cast out from royal family with
Some words they did not mince.
So he sat to type a letter but
The keyboard made him wince.
As the keyboard started typing
Ah, "A riddle!" he was convinced:

X the crying, time to focus,
If you are to be a king.
*Use **this word** to fix the chaos,*
For your people need this thing.

Since greed is quick to make a stain,
It's often tricky to maintain.
So C some wise men if you must,
And V their wisdom in those you trust.

Leaders wield it diligently,
To take it back you must be B.
Make mistakes that you may Z,
For you may lose it, can't you see?

A single word is A you need,
But many are robbed of it by greed.
Once you have it, A is well,
But can you keep it, time will tell.

Should you stumble, fumble, fail,
Y it all ... conquer, prevail!

#48

DIFFICULTY: 7

49

I must confess that I am impressed
With the success you've had in your passage of tests!
But this riddle at hand is unlike the rest,
So if you best it, I'll consider you blessed!
Do not stress if your eyes impede your progress,
For more may be less and your vision a mess.
If your eyes are deceiving, your ears may be best,
So I ask, will you translate the following, yes?

Want soup on eight I'm the air was up rinse S …

DIFFICULTY: 7

50

If this riddle is hard,
Then it must not be soft.
Though its letters are few
Its components are SOFT.
And I ask, can you find
What I seem to have doffed
In order to make a hard riddle just SOFT?

T T T F F S S _ _ O

DIFFICULTY: 7

Acknowledgments

A few months into the COVID pandemic, I met the woman of my dreams whom I now get to call my wife. We had just started dating when I created my first riddle (#41 in this book), and she became the first person to try each new riddle throughout the following years. She also became my top riddle-solver among all my family and friends—a title I hope she wears with pride. None of this would have been possible without her everlasting support and encouragement. For that and so much more, I love you and I thank you, Caline!

To Piglet (my little sister Stephanie), you have given me the much-needed, bountiful, constructive criticism—along with praise—on these riddles, helping me modify them into the best versions possible. I'll be the first to admit that you are actually better at solving riddles than I am. You have inspired me to delve into the artistic world with your own professional endeavor as the indie singer/songwriter known as Ellajay. (I encourage anyone reading this to check out her music on any streaming platform or visit ellajaymusic.com!)

To Mom and Dad, you have both been a guiding light throughout my life, offering a base of support and the right amount of encouragement to foster creativity. Mom, you especially encouraged me at a young age when I wrote my first poems and nurtured that side of me. I have no doubt it served as an early building block to this book of riddles. Dad, as one of the most brilliant people I know, having you light up with excitement upon solving a particularly tough riddle has given me immense joy and made this process that much more thrilling. The combination of that and your own feedback has been priceless.

To Mindy Kuhn, Erika Nein, and the staff at Warren Publishing, thank you for helping me publish this book and carrying me through each step of this process. You have made what would have otherwise been a daunting task feel very manageable, organized, and even fun. Thank you for connecting my riddles with the talented and incredible artwork of Alessandro D'urso, whose ability to turn each descriptive paragraph into a drawing is a skill I enviously admire.

Thank you to Emmanuel Lakis for his endless creativity in creating the accompanying website in all of its glory. This novel concept would have been impossible without his expertise.

Thank you to all of my friends who have solved some riddles, provided feedback, and offered their own words of encouragement.

And finally, thank you to all the readers and riddle-solvers out there. I hope you had as much fun solving these riddles as I did writing them!

Printed in the USA
CPSIA information can be obtained
at www.ICGtesting.com
LVHW062344050124
768284LV00005B/9

9 781960 146854